IMAGES
of America

ROUTE 15
THE ROAD TO HARTFORD

GOV. WILBUR L. CROSS. Wilbur L. Cross served as Connecticut's governor from 1931 to 1939. He graduated from Yale University twice, receiving his bachelor of arts degree in 1885 and his doctorate in 1889. Prior to accepting the nomination for governor as a Democrat, Cross was dean of the Yale Graduate School for 14 years. The Wilbur Cross Parkway and Wilbur Cross Highway are named for him.

IMAGES
of America

ROUTE 15
THE ROAD TO HARTFORD

Larry Larned

ARCADIA
PUBLISHING

Published by Arcadia Publishing
Charleston, South Carolina

Library of Congress Catalog Card Number: 2002105491

For all general information contact Arcadia Publishing at:
Telephone 843-853-2070
Fax 843-853-0044
E-mail sales@arcadiapublishing.com
For customer service and orders:
Toll-Free 1-888-313-2665

Visit us on the Internet at www.arcadiapublishing.com

GLASTONBURY CENTER, 1923. A shiny 1923 Buick is on display in the Hartford Buick showroom window. The fork to the left is the New London Turnpike. The fork to the right is Main Street. Main Street eventually became an improved state highway numbered Route 15. Old Route 15 was renumbered Route 17 during 1948, when the 117-mile ribbon of road including the Wilbur Cross Parkway and Wilbur Cross Highway were renumbered Route 15.

CONTENTS

ACKNOWLEDGMENTS

Heartfelt thanks go to those who assisted in this effort, especially Donna Abbott, Jim Fallon, Andree Larned, Malcolm and Betty-Lou Mitchell, Rob Moore, Carmel Owens, and Bruce Wood. The following organizations were most helpful in allowing access to photographs and archival resources: Roads and Streets Magazine, the Connecticut Society of Civil Engineers, the state of Connecticut, the Connecticut Historical Society, and the Hartford Courant.

THE CHARTER OAK BRIDGE, 1942. The Charter Oak Bridge is shown under construction from the East Hartford bank of the Connecticut River. The American Bridge Company is preparing to erect the final steel girders for completing the bridge superstructure from Hartford to East Hartford. When it was completed, the bridge was a vital section of the Route 15 highway built from Greenwich to Union.

RURAL CONNECTICUT, 1947. The Wilbur Cross Highway was constructed through rural eastern Connecticut, enabling residents in small towns better access to Hartford. Its main purpose, however, was to speed out-of-state traffic headed for destinations north and east of Boston through Connecticut, earning Connecticut the distinction of being a "pass-through state."

Dedicated to James H. MacDonald.

JAMES H. MACDONALD, PIONEER OF HIGHWAYS. On August 30, 1933, a crowd gathered at a roadside park on U.S. Route 44, located on the western slope of Talcott Mountain in Avon, Connecticut. The occasion honored James H. MacDonald, the first Connecticut State Highway Department commissioner. As the crowd looked on, a granite shaft with a bas-relief panel portrait in James MacDonald's likeness was dedicated. MacDonald was the father of the national "Good Roads Movement." He formulated national highway policy and favored connecting state road fragments into longer trunk-line routes. His philosophy was continued in 1948, when the Merritt and Wilbur Cross Parkways, the Berlin Turnpike, the Hartford Bypass, the Charter Oak Bridge, and the Wilbur Cross Highway were numbered Route 15. MacDonald's early leadership enabled the Connecticut State Highway Department to attain national prominence for its state highway system. The Connecticut State Highway Department, founded during 1895,was the third state highway agency in the nation.

8

One

PARKWAY MAGIC

Parkways became part of the American consciousness during 1924, when the Bronx River Parkway was constructed through the Bronx and lower Westchester County, New York. Other parkways quickly followed, including the Hutchinson River, Cross County, Saw Mill, and Taconic, but the Merritt Parkway became the charmer of them all. Fully opened to traffic during 1940, the Merritt's character was influenced by the 19th-century city-beautiful style. This style was popular during a period of American road-building history when attention was devoted to linking urbanized regions with graceful highways built through natural surroundings.

As construction progressed on the Merritt Parkway, a project intended to alleviate congestion on U.S. Route 1, Connecticut State Highway Department planners turned their attention to the next link in Connecticut's parkway system—the Wilbur Cross Parkway. Studies conducted during the late 1920s and early 1930s indicated serious traffic congestion between New Haven and Hartford on U.S. Route 5. A portion of this traffic was finding its way to Boston while avoiding the tortuous shoreline route of U.S. Route 1, suggesting that an improved road to Boston could become a future highway route. With these concerns in mind and the Merritt Parkway project under way, Connecticut legislators voted to construct the Wilbur Cross Parkway all the way to the Massachusetts state line at Union, Connecticut. This legislation also called for the Wilbur Cross Parkway to pass around Hartford, with one river crossing seven miles below the city and another river crossing above the city. Both the devastation of the 1936 flood of the Connecticut River in Hartford, which had partially isolated the city, and the realization that the congested Bulkeley Bridge was the sole river crossing between the cities of Hartford and East Hartford forced the legislature again to study the Wilbur Cross Parkway route.

The legislature passed a bill in 1939 to finance the planned Wilbur Cross Parkway by charging tolls on the nearly finished Merritt Parkway. This legislation included building a new bridge across the Connecticut River in Hartford—the Charter Oak Bridge. The same legislation postponed the construction of the new bridge below Hartford and specified a temporary merge of the Wilbur Cross Parkway into U.S. Route 5 north of Meriden. This "temporary" connection was a political victory for the business interests along the Berlin Turnpike, located just north of the parkway merge to U.S. Route 5.

The Milford Parkway was authorized during 1941. The two-mile section of the Wilbur Cross Parkway joining the toll station with U.S. Route 1 was renamed the Milford Parkway with its own set of distinctive bridges designed by George Dunkelberger. With a bold stroke, the legislature guaranteed the creation of a new route through Connecticut that emphasized parkway design at the southern end.

On November 1, 1949, Gov. Chester Bowles of Connecticut cut a ribbon at one end of the West Rock Tunnel to open the final eight-mile section of road from Greenwich to Union.

THE END OF THE HUTCH, THE BEGINNING OF THE MERRITT. Motorists driving into Connecticut on New York's Hutchinson River Parkway were greeted with this view of a manicured landscape during 1946. Merritt Parkway landscape architects paid particular attention to blending new vegetation with existing natural growth.

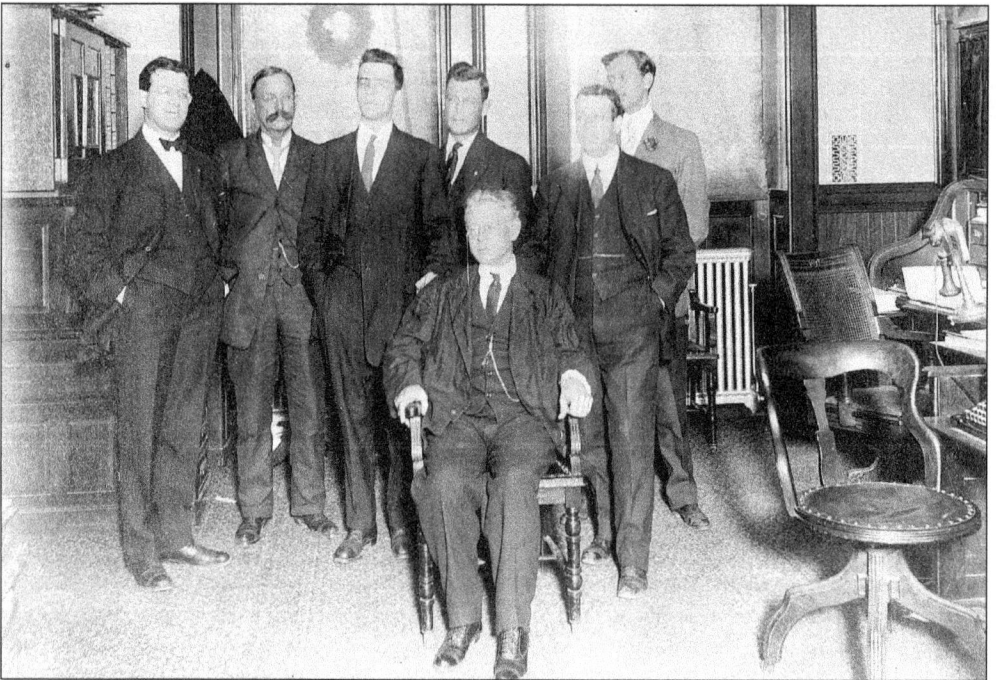

CONNECTICUT STATE HIGHWAY DEPARTMENT LEADERSHIP. Commissioner James H. MacDonald is shown with his senior Connecticut State Highway Department managers during 1907. The department had just completed a study identifying a workable system of interconnected roads for the state. The proposal was passed by the Connecticut legislature during 1913. It established 14 trunk-line routes connecting hundreds of road segments. A similar proposal established Route 15 during 1948.

RIPPLES CUT, WINTER 1935. This section of the Merritt Parkway was referred to as Ripples Cut. Located within one mile of the New York–Connecticut state line, the Ripples Cut section of the Merritt Parkway provides parkway historians with dramatic comparisons of the works of man and the forces of nature. In the distance, a palatial estate can be seen.

RIPPLES CUT. Dramatic evidence of a landscape design is apparent in this 1938 scene. Trees and shrubs have provided a parkway environment according to a landscape plan prepared by Connecticut State Highway Department landscape architects. The estate seen in the previous photograph has become invisible.

11

PROMOTING THE OPEN ROAD. The Shell Oil Company sponsored this national magazine advertisement in 1941. The theme "Roads of Tomorrow" captures the imagination, and relief is offered from driving U.S. Route 1, nicknamed the "Roaring Road." The Merritt Parkway was constructed as a parallel road for relieving the congested U.S. Route 1. In time, it became a segment of the much longer Route 15.

HEADED WESTBOUND. A 1950 Packard is shown leaving the Greenwich tollhouse after paying a 20¢ toll during the spring of 1962. The tollhouse, built in 1940, was a prominent feature of the Merritt Parkway. The tollbooths and administration building were constructed of rustic wood. The booth canopies were supported with stripped logs and roofed with hand-split cypress shingles.

BRIDGE CONSTRUCTION. The Riversville Road Bridge is shown under construction during 1934. On May 23, 1934, Schuler Merritt delivered the keynote speech for the Merritt Parkway groundbreaking ceremony at this site. Eighteen years later, a parkway benefactor transferred seven acres of land abutting the parkway between this location and Round Hill Road to the state.

DEPRESSION ERA FUNDING. The Riversville Road Bridge was one of only a few Merritt Parkway bridges constructed with Work Projects Administration funding. The Merritt Parkway was largely financed with a $15 million Fairfield County bond issue. County financing of roads in Connecticut is highly unusual. However, county financing for the Merritt Parkway enabled county residents greater participation in how the parkway was designed.

PARKWAY ENVIRONMENT. The completed Riversville Road Bridge is shown in Greenwich during late 1935. The bridge is contrasted with the long fill slope extending to a natural tree line. This carefully planned and executed environment exemplified the relationship of the parkway roadway to its surrounding parklike ambiance.

THE QUEEN OF PARKWAYS. Looking west from Round Hill Road in 1941, this view shows light traffic moving easterly along the Queen of Parkways. New plantings of dogwood, birch, oak, and mountain laurel have started to blend with native growth. This pleasing harmony between the works of man and the healing forces of nature earned the parkway many admirers.

15

ARCHITECTURAL DIVERSITY. A 1937 Oldsmobile passes through the Lake Avenue underpass in Greenwich. Referred to as the Grapes of Wrath bridge, it was constructed during 1940, two years after this section of the Merritt was opened to traffic. The bridge incorporates a blend of architectural elements—stone-faced abutments and a superstructure faced with trellises of cast malleable iron.

WINTER PEACE. A wisp of snow blows across the nearly completed Merritt Parkway during the winter of 1938 in Greenwich. Ancient stone walls give testimony to the former agricultural use of the land now occupied by the Merritt Parkway. The center-island pinch effect is very apparent at the Stanwich Road underpass. This type of design was intended to reduce the bridge's span length, a cost-saving measure.

16

BUTTERNUT HOLLOW ROAD. Yes, exit 30 did exist. This 1947 view shows vintage automobiles negotiating the hairpin curve on Butternut Hollow Road in Greenwich just before entering the Merritt Parkway. It was eliminated as a grade crossing with stop signs during 1955, when the center park strip was filled, but remained as an entrance only to the parkway. After a series of accidents, the entrance was finally closed.

PLEASING HARMONY. The Rocky Craig Road underpass was originally referred to as the Guinea Road Bridge. It was constructed in Stamford and faced with stone as part of a land-acquisition agreement. The structure's graceful design and use of natural materials reflects a Merritt Parkway design goal—to blend manmade materials with those of nature.

THE OPEN ROAD. A 1947 Buick and a 1948 Dodge are visible during typical 1947 driving conditions on the Merritt Parkway. Connecticut State Highway Department engineers designed the parkway from 1934 to 1940. Over its 38 miles of length, there were 12 major grading contracts, 13 major paving contracts, and 52 separate major bridge contracts employing thousands of workers.

HIGHWAY GEOMETRY. Parkway mathematics are evident in this 1951 view of a typical uphill, downhill curved alignment on the Merritt Parkway. In accordance with American highway design principles, the horizontal curves are circular with constant radii while the vertical curves are parabolic. The two mathematical relationships combine to produce a smooth and flowing appearance.

FRAMED TRAFFIC. As a 1948 Buick and a 1948 Dodge pass through an ivy-covered underpass on the Merritt Parkway, a stranded motorist waits for assistance in the distance. Being stranded on the Merritt Parkway was no fun, particularly at night. The roadway was not illuminated, and headlights had a tendency of becoming swallowed up in the darkness. Waiting for assistance meant waiting for a state police patrol.

WORLD WAR II TOLL STATION. The New Canaan state maintenance garage served as the site for collecting tolls from commercial trucks carrying explosives and munitions during World War II. In order to use the parkway for this purpose, special ramps were built where needed to route trucks around low-clearance underpasses. This special wartime use of the Merritt Parkway extended from June 15, 1943, to August 18, 1945.

SELECTING A STYLE. Prior to choosing a bridge façade on the Merritt Parkway, George Dunkelberger personally visited the site and sketched four different proposals. He believed a bridge should blend with its location. Accounting for existing contours and historic features were important considerations for his design decisions. The Lapham Avenue underpass in New Canaan is shown during 1941.

MARVIN RIDGE ROAD. Originally called the Weed Avenue underpass, this structure is considered one of the most beautifully designed bridges on the Merritt Parkway. Constructed during 1940 and costing just $25,976, this bridge was a favorite of its designer, George Dunkelberger. Featuring a classical Wedgewood style with a niched Wedgewood blue wall behind each white urn, the bridge presents a crisp image.

CLOSED TO TRAFFIC. This section of the Merritt Parkway in Norwalk was in disaster mode following hurricane flooding on October 16, 1955. Employees of the Leake & Nelson Steel Erection Company are setting a military Bailey bridge in place over the collapsed Silvermine River Bridge. The rigid-frame concrete arch bridge, built during 1938, extended 100 feet under the parkway.

PARKWAY CRITICS. Although many considered the Merritt Parkway a beautiful road, others criticized its design. A New York landscape architect called the Merritt a glorified roller coaster. Gilmore Clarke, designer of the Hutchinson River Parkway, stated the Merritt was "extravagant in construction and antique in design." These comments were attributed by some to professional jealousy.

22

A PARKWAY OASIS. This scene includes the dual gasoline stations located in Fairfield operated by Gulf Oil Corporation during 1946. In keeping with aesthetic sensitivity, large roadside "lollypop" signs were prohibited. Gulf, Cities Service, Atlantic, Flying A, and Mobil were among the companies who operated parkway gasoline stations. A percentage of sales was returned to the Connecticut State Highway Department for road maintenance.

WORTHY OF THE NATIONAL REGISTER. A Buick Roadmaster of 1950s vintage is heading eastbound on the Merritt Parkway during 1957. The road is shown resurfaced with asphalt. Following years of debate, the Merritt Parkway was nominated for and placed on the National Register of Historic Places effective April 17, 1991.

AUGUST 1948. Traffic is moving smoothly on the Merritt Parkway at the Newtown–Long Hill interchange. This scene shows a 1947 Pontiac approaching the camera. Parkway improvements made during 1955 included easing the turning radii at the exit and entrance ramps. As traffic volumes increased on the parkway, it became necessary to update features affecting safety.

PARKWAY ARCHITECT. George Dunkelberger is shown with his wife, Anna. Educated at Drexel Institute in Philadelphia and trained as an architect in the U.S. Navy, George Dunkelberger possessed superb artistic abilities. He drew equally well with both hands, played any musical instrument offered, and was adept at telling stories. He was the site coordinator for the Merritt and Wilbur Cross Parkway bridges.

PARKWAY MATURITY. As traffic volumes grew on the Merritt Parkway, the plantings did too. This view, taken during 1948, eight years after the parkway was opened, clearly shows the planned foliage beginning to mature along the traveled portion of the highway. As postwar budgets became tighter and priorities shifted to the Interstate Highway Program, less funding was made available to maintain 38 miles of landscaping on the parkway.

THE CONNECTICUT STATE HIGHWAY DEPARTMENT CELEBRATION BRIDGE. The James Farms Road underpass is a favorite among Merritt Parkway aficionados. Completed during 1940 and featuring a pair of disembodied wings created by the sculptor Edward Ferrari, this structure is the final underpass on the Merritt Parkway. Each abutment face carries a cameo with the letters CHD.

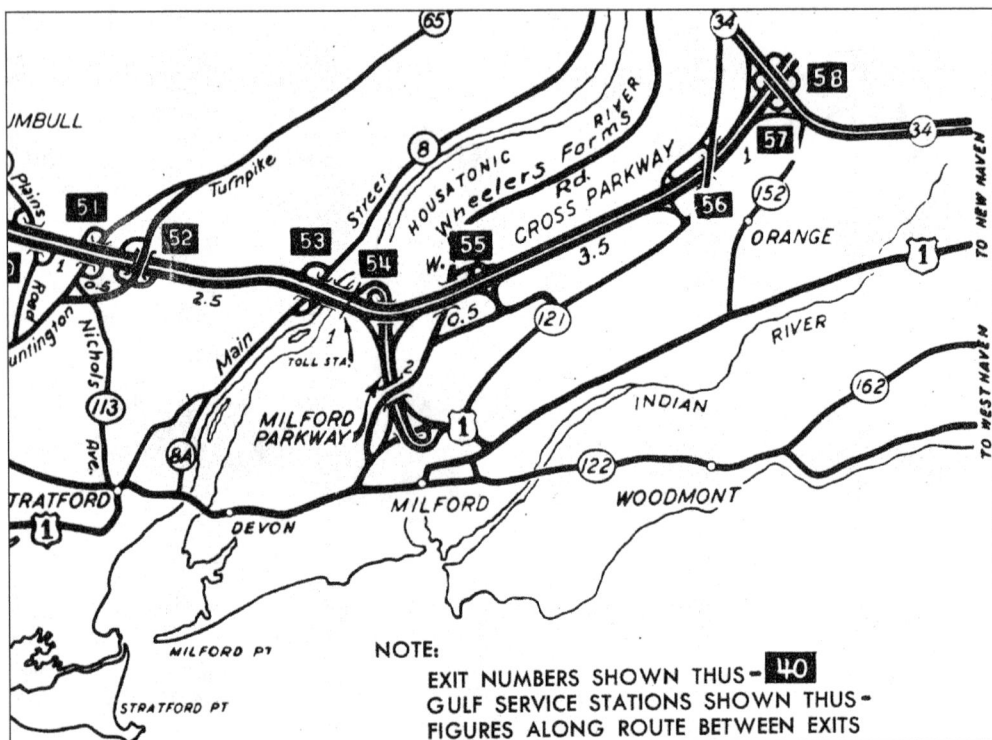

THE MILFORD PARKWAY. When revised planning for the Merritt Parkway included a bridge over the Housatonic River, a need arose for routing traffic to U.S. Route 1. The U.S. Route 1 connection became the Milford Parkway, barely two miles long, as shown on this Gulf Oil map.

BRIDGING THE MILFORD PARKWAY. Upon naming the southern appendage to the Wilbur Cross Parkway the Milford Parkway, under Special Act 99 during 1941, Connecticut gained a third parkway. Although only two miles long, the Milford Parkway contained five bridges. One of the most notable is the rigid-frame bridge over U.S. Route 1. This bridge is covered with architectural concrete panel facings normally used on buildings.

26

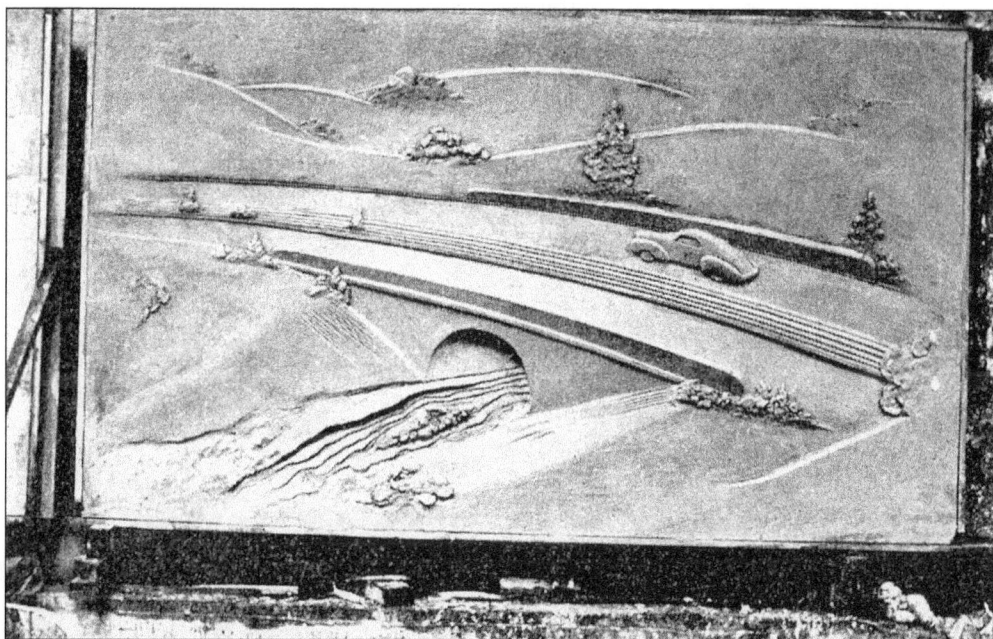

CLAY MODEL. Prior to a panel being cast in concrete, a clay model must be made to create a form from which the image is cast. This close-up view shows the clay model for panels on the Milford Parkway–U.S. Route 1 bridge. Originally referred to as the Milford Cutoff, the Milford Parkway retained its name until Interstate 95 opened in 1958. It then became the Milford Connector and gained another bridge with connections to Interstate 95.

THE MILFORD PARKWAY OVER U.S. ROUTE 1. This construction photograph shows workers placing a manufactured architectural panel on the U.S. Route 1 bridge during 1941. The panels were cast by the Dextone Company of New Haven, Connecticut. The modeled surfaces were cast integrally with the plain face of the panels that were two inches thick.

THE MILFORD TOLLHOUSE. Tolls at Milford marked the beginning of the Wilbur Cross Parkway, just east of the Housatonic River Viaduct. From 1939 to 1989, four toll stations were operated on Route 15. The three parkway tolls, including Wallingford, were removed during 1988. The main canopy section of the tolls was moved and preserved. It is displayed at Booth Park in Stratford. The single booth to the left is on display at the Henry Ford Museum and Greenfield Village.

FLAMING WHEELS. The Grassy Hill Road underpass was constructed on the Wilbur Cross Parkway during 1941. Located in Orange, this structure features an ornament depicting a flaming wheel on the top of each pier. When constructed, the area behind each wheel was painted red. George Dunkelberger designed the bridge and the ornaments. He was very disappointed with the ornaments and felt "they weren't so hot."

TRAVELING THE WILBUR CROSS PARKWAY. Among the automobiles heading northeast through Orange is a 1947 Plymouth, a 1948 Studebaker, and a 1947 Plymouth convertible. Unlike the Merritt Parkway, with its alignment rising and falling across ridges and valleys, the Wilbur Cross parkway alignment is fairly level, running mostly parallel to ridges and valleys

DERBY AVENUE. The Derby Avenue underpass and its interchange with the Wilbur Cross Parkway in Orange was opened to traffic on Christmas Eve 1941. It is nicknamed the Yale Bridge, and its design and detailing reflect the architecture and character of buildings on the Yale University campus. Speculation exists that Yale engineering students collaborated with Connecticut State Highway Department staff engineers during its design phase.

OVER THE HILL. This photograph, taken during 1950, looks south from the West Rock Tunnel portal toward Woodbridge to the right and New Haven to the left. Construction of the Wilbur Cross Parkway was financed with tolls collected on the Merritt Parkway.

TWIN BORES. The Wilbur Cross Parkway is shown under construction on May 27, 1949. This view, taken from Fountain Street in New Haven, shows the parkway construction extending to the twin bores of the West Rock Tunnel. Above the tunnel is West Ridge Rock Park, originally operated by the city of New Haven and later transferred to the state of Connecticut as a state park.

30

WEST PORTAL HEADING. Construction workers are drilling horizontal blast holes for the first phase of the tunnel excavation. Using compressed-air drills mounted on two drilling jumbos, the workers will load the drill holes 12 feet deep with Hercules Gelamite No. 2 dynamite and set off the blast. Following a blast on July 1, 1948, a rockfall occurred inside the tunnel, killing a shift boss named Meade. A bronze tablet in his honor is mounted on the west portal face.

TUNNEL RIBS. As blasted rock was removed from the tunnel, a process called mucking, curved I-beams—referred to as ribs—were placed to support the tunnel ceiling. The 1,202 ribs used in the West Rock Tunnel were fabricated, shaped, and shipped to the tunnel site by the Commercial Stamping and Shearing Company of Youngstown, Ohio. The ribs were bolted as four-piece frames and erected as the jumbos moved forward in the tunnel.

DAYLIGHT. The eastbound bore of the twin-bore West Rock Tunnel connects daylight at each end during December 1948. Artificial lighting illuminates the right-hand wall, and steel ribbing lines the bore from end to end. When completed, the tunnel was lined with concrete and faced with ceramic tile. A ventilation shaft was constructed from the mountaintop 180 feet to the tunnel roof line centered between the two bores.

HOLING THROUGH. November 8, 1948, was a memorable day for the West Rock Tunnel project. Construction workers and engineers gaze at the pile of rock resulting from a blast of 648 pounds of dynamite set off by Governor Shannon and witnessed by 300 people. The blast holed through the northbound tube. The steel lining placed from the opposite end is visible in the photograph.

32

RING STONES. The north end of the West Rock Tunnel is shown in May 1949. Ring stones of Vermont granite are shown being placed at each portal entrance. The finished stone faces were designed by George Dunkelberger, architect for the Merritt and Wilbur Cross Parkway bridges. Blasting at the tunnel site was monitored by Dr. L. Don Leete of Harvard University.

FINISH WORK. Stonemasons are shown completing the ring stones on the West Rock Tunnel north portal. Following completion of this task, work will proceed on facing the rough concrete tunnel portal with random ashlar stonemasonry. Additional stonemasonry was placed on the sides of the octagonal ventilation house located 180 feet above the tunnel.

THE TUNNEL OF LOVE. The West Rock Tunnel became the namesake for the movie *The Tunnel of Love*, starring Doris Day and Richard Widmark. Portions of the romantic comedy were filmed during 1950 on the southern approach to the tunnel. The movie's theme song, "Have Lips, Will Kiss in the Tunnel of Love," was sung by Doris Day.

CONSTRUCTION IMPACT. The Wilbur Cross Parkway and West Rock Tunnel project drastically changed the landscape shown in this photograph. Former farmland has been covered with fill, much of it spoil from the West Rock Tunnel. A new interchange serves the area, spread over acres of open land. The building being constructed to the right of the tunnel is the future home for the Connecticut State Highway Department District 3 Headquarters. This area is attractive and close to the only state highway tunnel in New England.

THE RUSTIC LOOK. A shingle-edged sign in the median of the Wilbur Cross Parkway between exits 64 and 63 advises motorists that Cities Service gas is available one mile ahead. Signing on Connecticut parkways was carefully controlled and well maintained. Very little parkway signing was illuminated, but the signs were covered with green Reflexite and lettered with white gothic characters.

NEW ENGLAND THEME. A 1948 Studebaker is being refueled at the North Haven gasoline station. This photograph, taken during 1950, shows the station attendant checking the oil. At this time, Atlantic gasoline is selling for 27¢ per gallon for regular and 29¢ per gallon for high test. The gasoline stations on the Wilbur Cross Parkway were similar to those on the Merritt Parkway.

BLOCKED DESIGN. Vintage automobiles pass through the State Street underpass in North Haven on the Wilbur Cross Parkway. Designed as a simple span structure, the bridge is a study in Frank Lloyd Wright blocked design, particularly its wing walls and center pier. This underpass contrasts with the curved surfaces of the Bishop Street underpass in the distance.

36

Two

GASOLINE ALLEY

Just north of the point where the Wilbur Cross Parkway ends and joins U.S. Route 5, the Berlin Turnpike begins as Gasoline Alley, or did during the golden fifties. This section in the Route 15 ribbon stretching from Greenwich to Union was one of the great neon capitals of the Northeast. Extending for 11 miles between the end of the Wilbur Cross Parkway and the Hartford Bypass in Wethersfield, the Berlin Turnpike was lined with 200 business establishments, including diners, dairy bars, hot dog stands, motels, drinking places, bowling alleys, dancing halls, petting zoos, and scores of gas stations. At least 20 traffic signals lined Gasoline Alley, intended to control four lanes of stop-and-go traffic.

The Berlin Turnpike rivaled U.S. Route 46 in Patterson, New Jersey, and U.S. Route 1 in Saugus, Massachusetts. During rush hour, it was an exhausting midpoint on the drive between New York and Boston. Business owners' livelihoods depended on travelers driving from the end of the Wilbur Cross Parkway, purchasing services on the Berlin Turnpike, and continuing to the Wilbur Cross Highway east of Hartford and on to U.S. Route 20 in Massachusetts.

Well-known businesses on the strip included the Cricket, Wonder Bar, and Puritan Maid restaurants, the Olympia Diner, Tina's Parkway Diner, Uncle Ezra's Hotdogs, two Howard Johnsons, and a Red Coach Grill. A landmark business was Freda Farms. Until World War II, Freda Farms was contained in a building shaped like an oversized cardboard ice-cream container. Mounds of pink ice cream with spoons protruded from the roof. Freda Farms put the Berlin Turnpike on the map as the concrete duck had along Route 24 near Riverhead, New York.

The early threat of bypassing the Berlin Turnpike with the Wilbur Cross Parkway Extension never materialized. The Turnpike Businessmen's Association maintained a strong lobby and fought all attempts for bypassing Gasoline Alley. On October 27, 1965, however, Interstate 91 opened between Meriden and Rocky Hill. Gasoline Alley was finally bypassed, and businesses along the Berlin Turnpike became victims of the interstate system.

THE ROUTE OF THE OLD HARTFORD–NEW HAVEN TURNPIKE. The Berlin Turnpike, at the time recently numbered U.S. Route 5, is shown during 1926, passing through fertile farmland in Berlin, Connecticut. Emerging land-use decisions in the town of Berlin assigned commercial development to the old turnpike road. By 1940, it had become a busy commercial route.

U.S. ROUTE 5 IS PAVED. A newly paved Berlin Turnpike is shown constructed through the Berlin meadows during 1927. A wire rope cable has yet to be installed through the vintage concrete stanchions on the right. It was common practice to run separate utility lines on either side of the road—one for electric and one for telephone.

FARMLAND BECOMES BILLBOARD SPACE. As agriculture declined, other uses were sought to gain income from the land. Farmers rented space to the billboard companies. A collection of billboards informing motorists of products and services lines both sides of the Berlin Turnpike during 1930 in Berlin. The billboards yielded to buildings of all descriptions by 1940. The Berlin Turnpike follows the path of the 1798 private Hartford–New Haven turnpike.

A ROAD MIRROR. A 1937 Hudson Terraplane reaches the crest of a hill on the Berlin Turnpike in Newington during 1941. The mirrored structure above the car is a Trafficscope designed to provide motorists ascending the hill from either direction with a view of the highway on the opposite side. Installed as an experiment at six sites in the United States during 1939, the scope contains a huge lens composed of rows of glass prisms. The Trafficscopes were erected on roads receiving federal aid funding for safety improvements.

TURNPIKE TRUCKING. A vintage tractor-trailer lumbers down the Berlin Turnpike in Berlin during 1946. To the right are Tina's Parkway Diner, a Mobil gas station, and a Howard Johnsons restaurant. This location is one mile north of the Wilbur Cross Parkway junction with the Berlin Turnpike.

A FUTURE ROADBED. A view taken during 1946 shows the Route 72 underpass over the widened Berlin Turnpike. In the foreground is the future right-of-way for the never constructed Wilbur Cross Parkway Extension. Without the parkway extension, Connecticut's role in contributing to a continuous parkway route from New York City ended at U.S. Route 5 in Meriden.

FUTURE CONSTRUCTION NEEDS. The original Berlin Turnpike shown southbound in the background is contrasted with the newly constructed Berlin Turnpike shown northbound during 1945. A postwar road-construction program included the reconstruction of the original southbound lanes to modern standards through Newington. The 1937 Terraplane is passing a 1941 Ford truck.

A CLASSIC FILLING STATION. Blinn's Tourist Court and Flying A Filling Station are shown during late 1945 on the Berlin Turnpike at the junction of Robbins Avenue in Newington. The Blinn family settled in Newington in the early 1700s.

FULL SERVICE. The Puritan Maid Restaurant was located in Berlin and featured chicken pies, fried clams, hamburgers, and fresh doughnuts. It was a favorite stopping place for parkway travelers. Puritan Maid offered one-stop service, advertising, "Fill your tummy and fill your tank."

THE WONDER BAR. This restaurant was a favorite Berlin Turnpike roadhouse for many years. Located in Berlin, it was enlarged numerous times and became a party spot for numerous organizations in the Hartford area. Vintage automobiles include a 1937 Ford, a 1936 Ford, a 1941 DeSoto, and a 1941 Chevrolet. To the right is the B & M Auto Repair Garage.

42

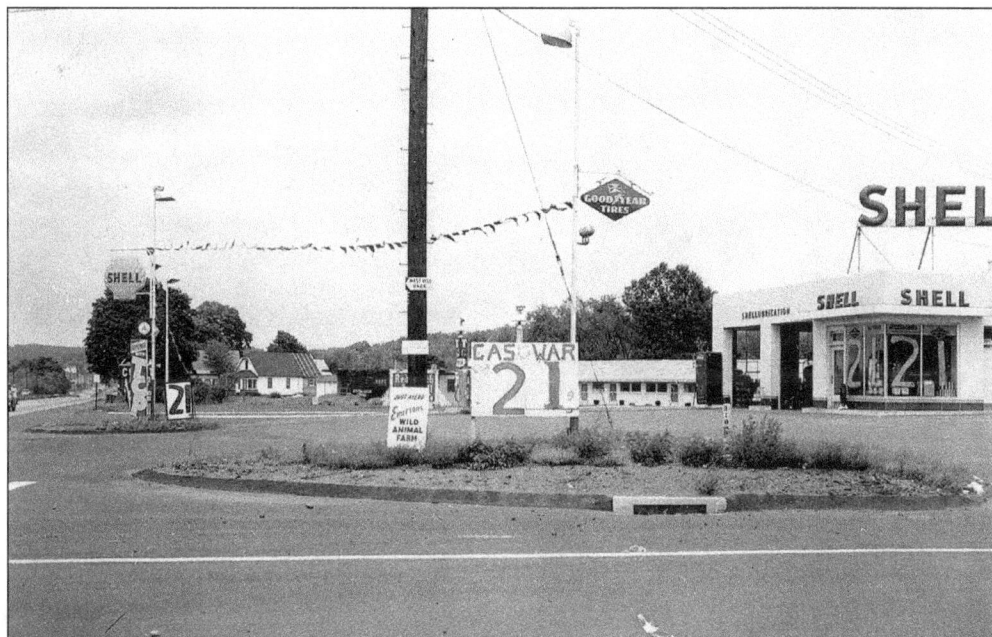

TURNPIKE GAS WARS. A Shell gasoline station advertises gasoline for 21¢ per gallon during 1954 on the Berlin Turnpike in Newington. Gas wars were common on the Berlin Turnpike as operators tried to capture motorists' attention on the turnpike while they drove to northern destinations. Locals cruised up and down Gasoline Alley, keeping a lookout for the best deal on gas.

TURNPIKE GULF. At its peak, Gasoline Alley boasted of 32 gas stations. This abundance of gas stations led to the turnpike's nickname of Gasoline Alley. By 1960, 40,000 automobiles a day jammed the Berlin Turnpike, and it gained another nickname, the Death Strip, as drag racers challenged the 20 traffic signals controlling 11 miles of four-lane highway.

THIRTY-SEVEN FLAVORS. Freda Farms was a landmark on the Berlin Turnpike for many years. It was originally located in a whimsical building shaped like an ice-cream box with a pink ice-cream roof. Freda Farms recognized that motorists headed to the Berlin Turnpike to purchase ice cream and gasoline. High Test was included among the featured flavors.

A LOOK DOWN THE PIKE. Traffic is light on the Berlin Turnpike during October 1945. To the left is Wayside Furniture in the midst of wartime closure. The grassy median of the turnpike stretches for miles toward Berlin. Two prewar tractor-trailers, the first a Federal, are headed northbound.

44

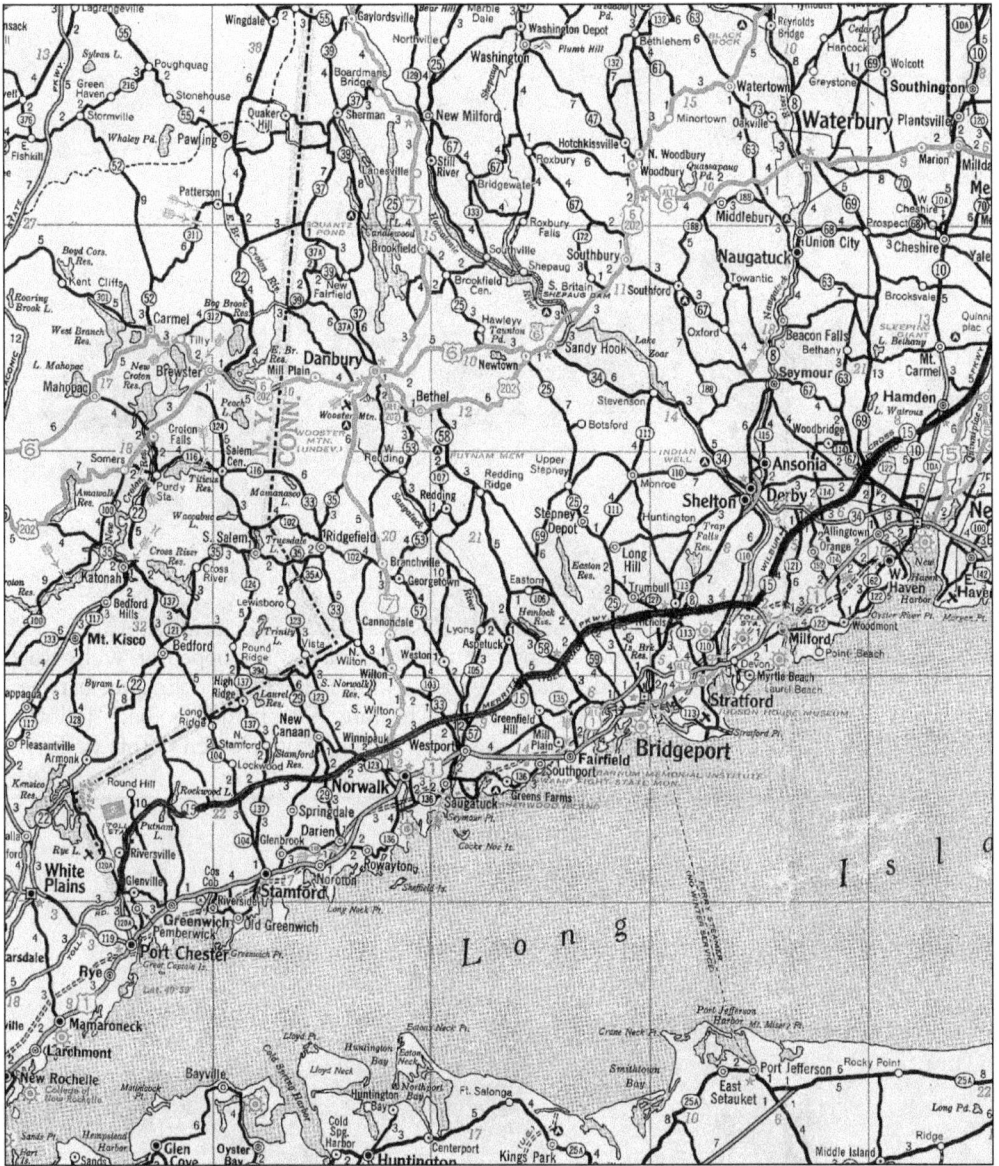

DRIVING FROM NEW YORK TO CENTRAL NEW ENGLAND. The southern end of Route 15 is shown extending from Greenwich to Wallingford. Motorists driving from New York and New Jersey used Route 15 as an alternate route to Boston and points in northern New England. Interstate 95 appears as a dashed line and is not yet constructed. Except for toll stations at Greenwich, Milford, and Wallingford, travel was unimpeded on Route 15 from Greenwich to Berlin. Until Interstate 95 was completed between New York and Boston, Route 15 was the primary tourist route through Connecticut. Economic interests along the route benefited from travelers purchasing gasoline, meals, and overnight accommodations.

VINTAGE VEHICLES AT WELLS ROAD. A pair of vintage vehicles is stopped at Wells Road and the Silas Deane Highway in Wethersfield. Wells Road became a busy connector between the Berlin Turnpike and the Silas Deane Highway. The rare 1942 Ford Woodie is followed by a 1947 Chevrolet. The strip of stores includes Silas Deane Drug, Doreen's, Tots & Teens, Edward's Men Shop, First National, and Silas Deane Sport Shop.

RURAL TRANQUILITY. This view, looking east in 1947 from the Berlin Turnpike, shows Wells Road (Route 175) extending to the Silas Deane Highway in Wethersfield. Its rural character was replaced with residential development within easy driving range of Hartford.

46

Three

APPROACHING HARTFORD

When the Berlin Turnpike ends, it ends not as a road but as a linear place. The motorist is given the choice of continuing on Maple Avenue into Hartford or bearing right on Route 15 and continuing on the Hartford Bypass either to Hartford or over the Charter Oak Bridge. The Hartford Bypass was part of the plan to alleviate the volume of traffic passing through Hartford streets and heading for distant points outside the Hartford region. Highway planners also saw the need for better access to Connecticut's capital and, looking to the future, for some type of highway paralleling the Connecticut River to Windsor. The Hartford Bypass included ramps at Wawarme Avenue designed to connect with the Park River Express Highway that was completed after World War II. In time, the Hartford Bypass became the South Meadows Expressway, and the Park River Express Highway became Connecticut River Boulevard.

The Hartford Bypass has some resemblance to a parkway, particularly its bridges, including the Ridge Road stone-faced underpass and the others with distinctive railing medallions designed by George Dunkelberger. The bypass, with parkway characteristics, also alleviated the jolt of Berlin Turnpike commercialism. The southern section of the bypass was constructed through a residential section of Wethersfield with a sizable bridge over the intersection of Jordan Lane and Wolcott Hill Road. George Dunkelberger, who lived steps away from the Jordan Lane Bridge, contributed his talents to the ornamentation applied to the fascia girders. Its central span, extending 120 feet, is actually suspended between a set of anchor spans and cantilever spans. The property to the northeast of the Jordan Lane Bridge would become the site for the Connecticut State Highway Department headquarters during 1959. Located at 24 Wolcott Hill Road, the complex was designed by Hartford architect Henry F. Ludorf.

After passing over the Wethersfield Avenue Bridge, the bypass changes character and enters Hartford's south meadows. Constructed on top of the Hartford flood-control dike, the bypass was built through a semi-wilderness during World War II. Following its construction with ramps at Maxim Road, a period of intense real estate speculation and development occurred to the east of the bypass. With the Connecticut River safely contained and a new arterial highway constructed, Hartford gained room for expansion to the southeast.

THE NEW ROUTE U.S. ROUTE 5. This 1946 scene shows the Hartford Bypass just north of the Berlin Turnpike's northerly terminus near the Wethersfield-Hartford town line. The two-span, rigid-frame bridge carries the bypass over old U.S. Route 5 (Maple Avenue). Its abutments are faced with precast panels similar to those used on the Milford Parkway bridges.

THE JORDAN LANE BRIDGE. The most prominent structure on the Hartford Bypass is the Jordan Lane Bridge at Wolcott Hill Road in Wethersfield. Located two miles south of the Charter Oak Bridge, the Jordan Lane Bridge weighs 870 tons and, when it was constructed in 1942, it was the largest all-welded structure built in Connecticut. George Dunkelberger, who designed its architectural elements, lived next door at 92 Wolcott Hill Road.

THE CHARTER OAK BRIDGE STREET CONNECTIONS. The Connecticut State Highway Department (CHD) was recognized as a national leader regarding its fine roads and responsive public-relations efforts. During 1942, the department printed this map to educate drivers about routes connecting to the newly opened Charter Oak Bridge.

49

A ROUTE 15 LANDMARK. The Connecticut Highway Department Administration Building in Wethersfield is shown following its completion during 1959. Built adjacent to the Hartford Bypass at a cost of $3.3 million, the complex was wholly owned and maintained by the highway department. This was in contrast to other state facilities owned and maintained by the state public works department.

HEADQUARTERS. Located on Wolcott Hill Road and within sight of Route 15, the Connecticut Highway Department Administration Building housed the department's executive offices, engineering, planning, rights-of-way, traffic operations, and bureau of maintenance. Referred to as headquarters, the complex had a decidedly military and professional character under the leadership of Commissioner (Col.) Howard S. Ives.

50

RAIL CARS AND ROAD CARS. A small diesel-electric switch engine, No. 8083, owned by United Aircraft Corporation, pushes a string of tank cars loaded with heavy fuel oil into the powerhouse siding of Pratt and Whitney in East Hartford. A Divco milk truck idles at left as a 1936 Dodge and a 1948 Dodge wait their turn to pass. This portion of Main Street in East Hartford was signed Route 15 until the number was reassigned to the parkways, the Berlin Turnpike, the Hartford Bypass, the Charter Oak Bridge, and the Wilbur Cross Highway.

GLASTONBURY CENTER, 1930. The Hartford Buick showroom has become Boulevard Chevrolet Company, and Main Street is paved as Route 15. To the right is Franklin Drug. Trolleys operated by the Hartford Street Railway ran on the track from Roaring Brook in South Glastonbury past this point in Glastonbury Center to Church Corners in East Hartford and into Hartford over the Bulkeley Bridge. Hales Farm peaches were shipped to Hartford and national markets along this line in special freight trolleys.

THE LONG COVERED BRIDGE. The Hartford Toll Bridge was constructed as the first substantial Connecticut River bridge during 1818, under the supervision of Ithiel Town of New Haven and Isaac Damon of Northampton, Massachusetts. When completed, this imposing covered bridge extended 974 feet from Hartford to East Hartford where its successor, the Bulkeley Bridge, now exists. The covered bridge contained a drawspan at its western end and carried two lanes

of opposing traffic. The overhead trusses carried 40 open-wire telephone circuits across the river. During 1890, horsecar tracks were added and electric trolley car service soon followed, extending from Hartford to Glastonbury. On May 17, 1895, a spectacular fire destroyed the bridge end-to-end.

THE BULKELEY BRIDGE. This was the third bridge constructed at the same location. Completed during 1908, it replaced the wood-covered Hartford Toll Bridge and its predecessor, the open timbered Hartford Bridge, which was destroyed by ice during 1818. The Bulkeley Bridge is a beautifully designed and crafted stone arch structure.

A BIRD'S-EYE VIEW. An aerial view of Hartford taken during 1958 shows World War II tract housing built for defense workers to the right. At the bottom, Route 15 crosses the Charter Oak Bridge to East Hartford. The newly opened Founders Bridge and the Bulkeley Bridge can be seen upstream.

NIGHT TRAFFIC. The Charter Oak Bridge toll plaza and tollhouse to the left are clearly seen in this night photograph taken during 1946. The plaza was equipped with 10 lanes to accommodate future traffic requirements. In this photograph, only one lane is open in each direction as a tractor-trailer heads eastbound into the night after paying its 20¢ toll.

CONNECTICUT RIVER BOULEVARD. Upon completion in 1947, the Park River Express Highway gained a new name—Connecticut River Boulevard. This photograph shows Colt's Firearms to the left, the boulevard with a bin wall retaining the Hartford Dike, and upstream the Bulkeley Bridge. Sixteen years later, the boulevard was gone. An elevated structure took its place, carrying Interstate 91.

A City Landscape. The Connecticut River Boulevard roadways to the left and right are ramps to and from Route 15 and the Charter Oak Bridge. Van Dyke Avenue and the New Haven Railroad are also visible to the left, with the Travelers Tower rising in the background. A fleeting view of the Connecticut River is visible before vehicles drop below the Hartford Dike.

Connecticut's Capital. The road to Hartford made Connecticut's capital more accessible to residents and legislators alike. Prior to the completion of Route 15 across the state, a trip to the capital often consumed two hours of road travel from Fairfield County and northeastern Connecticut. For this reason, the Route 15 projects received considerable support from legislators and voters.

Four

THE CHARTER OAK BRIDGE

Hartford, Connecticut, is a river city separated from its eastern neighbors and from Boston by the Connecticut River. Until 1942, when the Charter Oak Bridge was opened to traffic, Hartford's only road connection to the east was the Bulkeley Bridge, beautifully crafted of stone but insufficient to handle substantial automobile traffic. With the opening of the Merritt Parkway in 1940 and construction of the Wilbur Cross Parkway under way, the Connecticut legislature authorized a new bridge at Hartford to be named the Charter Oak Bridge and to be operated by the Hartford Bridge Commission.

The Charter Oak Bridge is an important link in the Route 15 ribbon of road from Greenwich to Union, Connecticut. Without the Charter Oak Bridge, the Merritt and Wilbur Cross Parkways, the Berlin Turnpike, the Hartford Bypass, and the Wilbur Cross Highway would have inundated Hartford with traffic congestion. When the Charter Oak Bridge opened to traffic in 1942, it provided another link in the new land route leading to Boston and points in central and northern New England. Hartford became a node in the travel patterns of millions, with its geographic location equidistant between New York and Boston.

George Dunkelberger, the Merritt Parkway architect and a resident of Wethersfield, was directed to design the decorative elements of the new bridge. His work included the four different cast medallions that graced the railings of the Charter Oak Bridge and the smaller bridges on the Hartford Bypass, which connected the Berlin Turnpike to the new bridge. Each medallion reflected a local theme—the famous Charter Oak, the historic old statehouse, the well-known East Hartford Congregational Church, and the airplanes powered with Pratt and Whitney engines, built by United Aircraft Corporation in East Hartford.

RIVER REFLECTION. The Connecticut River is absolutely still as its surface captures a reflection of the Charter Oak Bridge river piers and steel superstructure. Decorative elements cast into the pier caps and railings reflect George Dunkelberger's artistic and architectural talents.

THE SIGN OF THE CHARTER OAK. A meaningful logo for the Charter Oak Bridge was designed by the Hartford Bridge Commission. It was a common sight on roads leading to the Charter Oak Bridge and used on maps produced and distributed by the Hartford Bridge Commission and Connecticut State Highway Department.

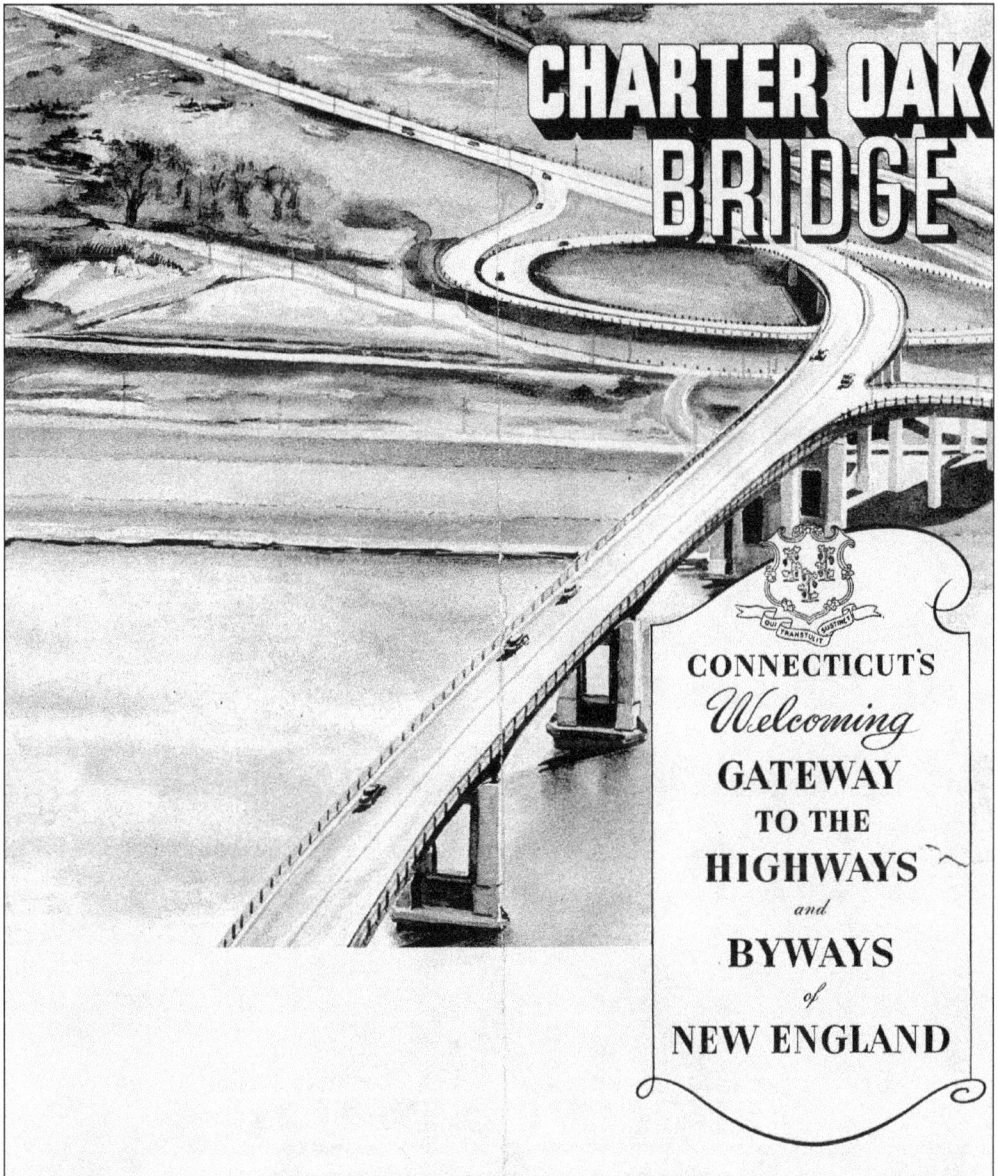

CHARTER OAK BRIDGE

CONNECTICUT'S
Welcoming
GATEWAY
TO THE
HIGHWAYS
and
BYWAYS
of
NEW ENGLAND

A GUIDE FOR MOTORISTS. An attractive brochure was printed during 1948 and distributed to motorists at the Charter Oak Bridge toll station. Its purpose was to promote the use of the Charter Oak Bridge by tourists. Route 15 became the favored route for vacation-bound tourists headed for northern New England. The Connecticut Turnpike (Interstate 95) and other interstate highways in Connecticut were not available for travel before 1958. The Charter Oak Bridge was promoted as the focal point of Connecticut's arterial highway system.

ROBERT D. OLMSTED. Robert D. Olmsted served as treasurer of the Hartford Bridge Commission, the agency responsible for the construction and operation of the Charter Oak Bridge. This arrangement continued until 1951, when the Connecticut State Highway Department assumed the administrative functions for the three toll bridges at Hartford, New London, and Old Saybrook.

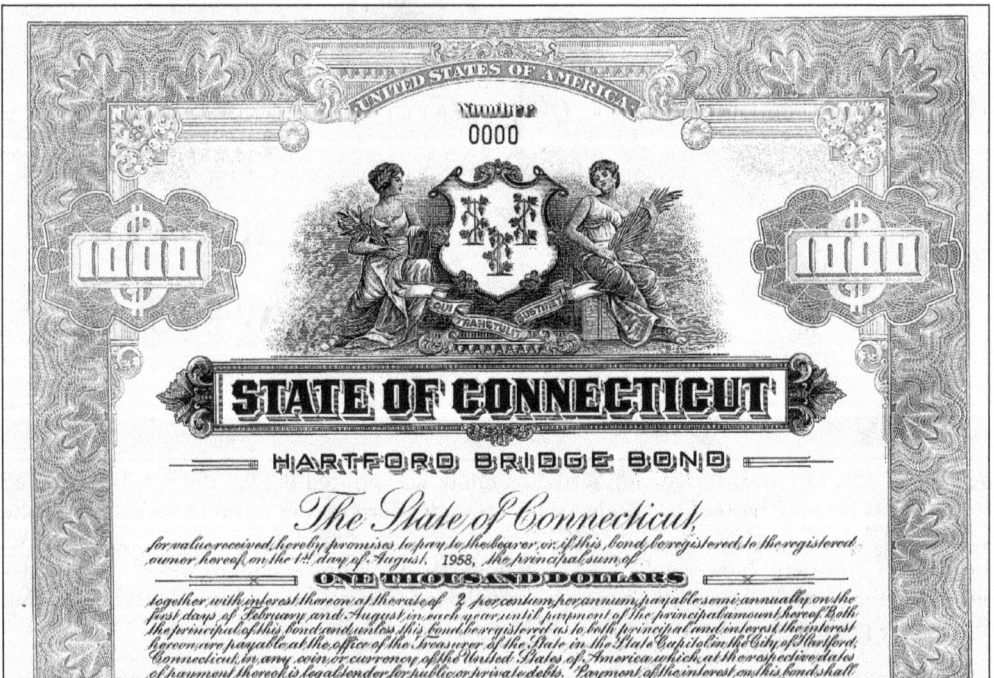

A HARTFORD BRIDGE BOND. Funds for building the Charter Oak Bridge were obtained through a bridge bond that raised $4.4 million, payable over 25 years using tolls and fee income. The first bond principal retirement payment was due on August 1, 1944. However, without sufficient funds from the bridge toll revenues to pay the amount owed, the general fund of the state was utilized to make the payment.

A PROPOSED BRIDGE. The Charter Oak Bridge had a would-be predecessor at the same location that was never built. Clarence Hudson, consulting engineer, was retained by an appointed bridge commission to study the need for a second bridge over the Connecticut River at Hartford. Referred to as the Connecticut River Bridge, it was designed by Robinson and Steinman, a prominent bridge engineering firm, in 1932.

TOWER DESIGN FOR CONNECTICUT RIVER BRIDGE AT HARTFORD
Architectural Design in the Colonial Spirit
Robinson & Steinman, Engineers.

PROPOSED CONNECTICUT RIVER BRIDGE AT HARTFORD
To be the first long-span bridge in Connecticut. Main span, 800 feet. Total length, two miles
Robinson & Steinman, Engineers.

A DREAM NEVER REALIZED. The Connecticut River Bridge was designed as a long-span suspension bridge, extending from Main Street at Silver Lane in East Hartford to Wyllys Street and Wethersfield Avenue in Hartford. Bids were received in March 1933. A low bid of $4.4 million was accepted, and construction was expected to start in due course. However, the banks were closed during the Great Depression, and no action was taken by the legislature until a new bridge commission was formed during 1939.

BUILDING THE CHARTER OAK BRIDGE. In this view looking toward Dutch Point, concrete piers for the Park River Express Highway ramp are shown left to right. Similar piers for the Charter Oak Bridge appear in the background. A dredging discharge pipe is transporting river sand to locations along the Hartford Dike. A widened dike was necessary to support the four-lane divided express highway. Within 20 years, Interstate 91 would occupy the same location.

TAKING A BREAK. Employees of the A.I. Savin Construction Company of Bloomfield, Connecticut, take a lunch break late in 1940 as work continues on forms for a bridge pier on the northwest viaduct portion of the Charter Oak Bridge. A light tower to the left provided illumination for extended working hours. A.I. Savin and the American Bridge Company were low bidders for the Charter Oak at $1,909,468.

DELIVERING EQUIPMENT. The tugboat *Sachem* heads downstream on the Connecticut River after dropping a barge-mounted crane at the Charter Oak Bridge construction site. In the background are the northwest viaduct piers needed to support the steel superstructure for carrying traffic from the Charter Oak Bridge to the capital area of Hartford.

RESIDENT ENGINEER. Howard S. Ives served as the resident engineer on the Charter Oak Bridge project. He became the Connecticut State Highway Department commissioner during 1959, a position he retained for 10 years. The Charter Oak Bridge was designed jointly by the firm of Robinson and Steinman and by engineers of the Connecticut State Highway Department.

QUALITY CONTROL. Connecticut State Highway Department construction inspectors perform a "slump test" on concrete being used in the bridge piers of the Charter Oak Bridge during 1941. A slump test determines consistency of the concrete, which is a measure of water content.

STEEL ERECTION. The erection of the steel superstructure for the Charter Oak Bridge continues during early spring of 1942. Work is proceeding from the Hartford shore to the east and over the Connecticut River.

OVER THE RIVER. A temporary steel bent supports steel girders being placed from the Hartford side of the Connecticut River. The bridge steel was fabricated in Pennsylvania and shipped to the Charter Oak Bridge site by rail. At the time of construction, the bridge was the largest steel-plate girder bridge in the world.

HIGH STEEL. At mid-river, a rocker span is being lowered into position 90 feet above the water. Ironworkers from California, Pennsylvania, New York, Rhode Island, Massachusetts, and Connecticut were employed on the project.

A DISASTROUS DAY. On December 4, 1941, just three days before Pearl Harbor, a construction accident at the Charter Oak Bridge site claimed the lives of 16 ironworkers. The toll included Jim Ward, a bridge-erection superintendent for the American Bridge Company who fell 80 feet to the ground. It was the worst loss of life in Hartford in 50 years.

SALVAGE. A barge-mounted crane has raised a portion of the fallen bridge-erecting crane from the Connecticut River. In all, 650 tons of bridge steel, lifting derricks, welding machines, air compressors, and 30 men fell to the water. Cal Robinson, a Connecticut State Highway Department construction inspector and accomplished swimmer, dove into the frigid waters and rescued eight men trapped in the wreckage. An inquiry determined that a portion of the Hartford Dike had slipped and weakened a temporary pile bent.

CORRECTIVE WORK. Ironworkers erect replacement steel between pier 12 on the Hartford shore to pier 13 in the Connecticut River, 272 feet away. A temporary pile-supported falsework pier with a steel cross bracing is visible in the photograph. Two falsework piers were used under each span following the December 4, 1941 accident. A steel piling is being raised for use in the second falsework pier.

VIADUCT CONSTRUCTION. Steel erection continues on the river span of the Charter Oak Bridge during June 1942. In the foreground, steel erection has been completed for the northwest viaduct, connecting the bridge to the Park River Express Highway, later named Connecticut River Boulevard. Within three months of this picture, the bridge was opened to traffic.

DECK PAVING. In this July 7, 1942 photograph, a crane-suspended concrete bucket places a load of fresh concrete on the deck-reinforcing steel of the Charter Oak Bridge. In the foreground is a finger joint allowing for expansion and contraction. On the right, carpenters build forms to contain deck steel and the concrete pavement.

OPPOSITE COLT FIREARMS. The Park River Express Highway is shown under construction. This segment of the Charter Oak Bridge project was suspended during World War II, with construction resuming in 1946. The flood-protection dike shown above, built following the great 1936 flood, was widened to support the Park River Express Highway. The Charter Oak Bridge is seen in the background.

LOOKING TOWARD DUTCH POINT. With the Charter Oak Bridge visible through the haze, construction continues during 1942 on widening the Hartford flood-control dike to the left of the metal bin wall. During 1940, while under construction, a section of the widened dike 1,000 feet long, seen in this photograph, collapsed into the river. This was regarded as the most likely cause of the construction accident that killed 16 ironworkers on December 4, 1941.

THE COMPLETED CHARTER OAK BRIDGE. The completed structure is shown extending from shore to shore during the winter of 1943. Three steel frames hang from the bridge, supporting navigation lights for marking the river channel. The dark figures are military personnel standing watch as the Connecticut River flows to the south.

69

Admit *Mr. William B. Griffin* and party

To the Dedication and Opening Exercises

of

CHARTER OAK BRIDGE

on Saturday, September Fifth, at 10 a. m.

East Plaza, East Hartford

GUEST

Charter Oak Bridge

PREPARATIONS FOR THE OPENING. This guest pass and vehicle windshield sticker are assigned to William B. Griffin for the dedication and ribbon-cutting ceremony of the Charter Oak Bridge, scheduled for September 5, 1942. William B. Griffin was named manager of the Charter Oak Bridge and related toll station. The toll complex was a small community, open 24 hours a day.

HENRY H. CONLAND CHAIRMAN	HENRY WOLCOTT BUCK SECRETARY	ROBERT D. OLMSTED TREASURER
RAYMOND A. JOHNSON	W. ROSS McCAIN	WILLIAM B. GRIFFIN MANAGER

STATE OF CONNECTICUT

HARTFORD BRIDGE COMMISSION

INVITATION

The Hartford Bridge Commission cordially invites you to attend the dedication exercises at the opening of the Charter Oak Bridge.

Saturday, September 5, 1942

There is enclosed a ticket of admission for yourself and party to the reserved area for guests and a card for your windshield that will admit you to the reserved parking area.

Invocation by Rt. Rev. Walter H. Gray. The exercises will be brief and informal with short talks by His Excellency, Hon. Robert A. Hurley, Governor; State Highway Commissioner Wm. J. Cox; and Chairman of the Hartford Bridge Commission, Henry H. Conland.

The ceremonies will take place on the east plaza in East Hartford and you may enter the official guest parking area from Main Street, East Hartford, at the northwest ramp to be designated by signs and attendants.

The speaking program will be broadcast and will start promptly at ten o'clock.

At the conclusion of the exercises, all invited guests under police escort may proceed west through the Toll Station over the Charter Oak Bridge and over the north lane to the intersection of Route 5 and return on the south lane to and over the bridge and through the Toll Station and east plaza and disperse.

Immediately after the passage of the official party, the bridge will be open to the public.

HENRY H. CONLAND,
Chairman

A PATRIOTIC INVITATION. Eight hundred invitations printed in red, white, and blue were extended to the Hartford–East Hartford community by the Hartford Bridge Commission. The commission was established to build and operate the Charter Oak Bridge as a distinct financial entity, although the Connecticut State Highway Department maintained the roadways and included them in the Route 15 network.

70

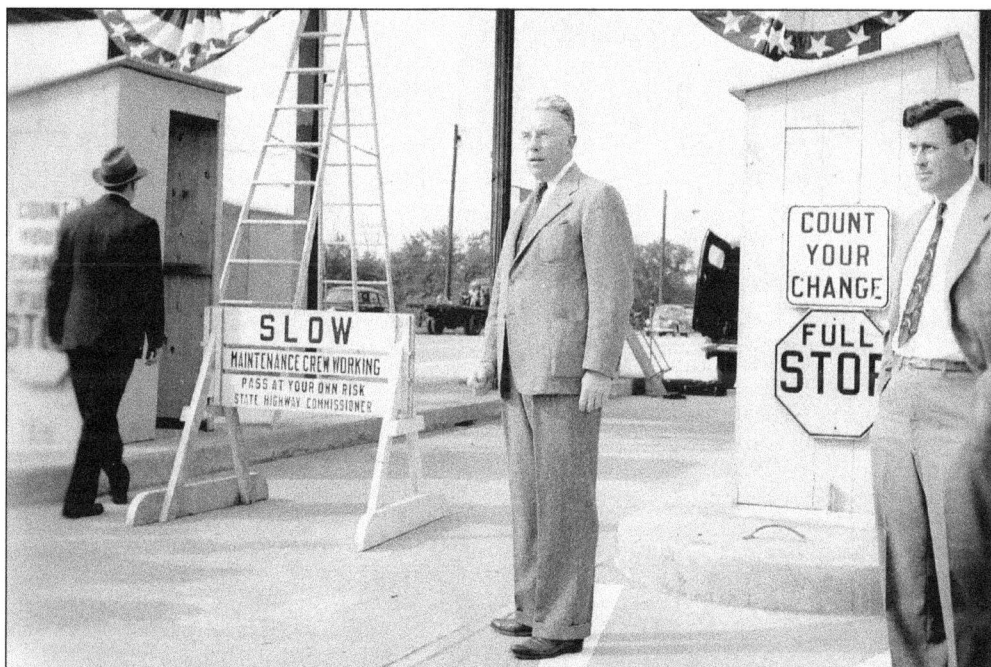

THE DEDICATION. The Charter Oak Bridge was dedicated and opened to traffic on September 5, 1942. William B. Griffin, manager of the Charter Oak Bridge, stands at center. Dignitaries included Gov. Robert Hurley and State Highway Commissioner William J. Cox. The dedication prayer was by Rt. Rev. Walter H. Gray, Episcopal suffragan bishop of Connecticut, who dedicated the bridge "to the service of the people of the state and the nation, a symbol of the many world differences which must be spanned before unity of mind and purpose can be attained."

GUARDING THE CHARTER OAK. A U.S. Navy sentry stands watch at the easterly approach to the newly opened Charter Oak Bridge during 1942. Until the conclusion of World War II, the sidewalks were closed to pedestrian traffic as a precaution against saboteurs who could drop explosives on maritime vessels.

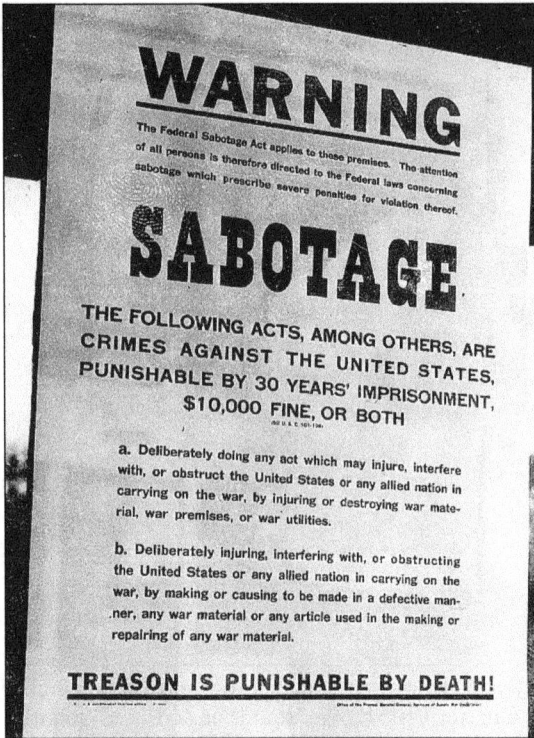

SABOTAGE WARNING. On its day of opening, the Charter Oak Bridge and the Hartford Bypass were placed on the strategic highway system established by the U.S. War Department. The bridge was guarded 24 hours a day by armed and deputized Connecticut State Highway Department employees. A military officer was assigned to the bridge and maintained an office in the toll station. The poster was placed in the window of each toll booth.

THE HARTFORD SKYLINE. This view, taken during 1945 from the Charter Oak Bridge, is looking upstream with the Travelers Tower in the center. Colt Firearms is shown to the left, with its distinctive onion dome. Construction has resumed on the Park River Express Highway, delayed by World War II material shortages. This length of road was built on top of the Hartford Flood Control Dike and in future years became the footprint for Interstate 91.

THE COMMISSION SECRETARY. Henry W. Buck of Wethersfield served as secretary of the Hartford Bridge Commission until January 6, 1951, when administrative authority for the Charter Oak Bridge was transferred to the Connecticut State Highway Department. (Roushon.)

THREE TRANSPORTATION MODES. A lone boxcar sits on the Valley Division of the New Haven Railroad as vintage automobiles travel Connecticut River Boulevard and ships unload cargo upstream from the Hartford Gas Company. This scene, taken during 1947, also includes the Bulkeley Bridge to the right.

THE HIDDEN RIVER. Hartford's Commerce Street Bridge is shown under construction during 1942. A plate girder design, it is passing over the future Park River Express Highway, later named the Conland-Whitehead Highway. The outline of the Park River Conduit, through which the confined waters of the Park River pass, is clearly seen below the bridge.

THREE LEVELS. The completed Commerce Street Bridge is the top level of three tiers. Beneath the bridge is the Conland-Whitehead Highway, and beneath the highway are the rushing waters of the Park River. The Commerce Street Bridge was one of three structures built over the Park River Express Highway for the Charter Oak Bridge project.

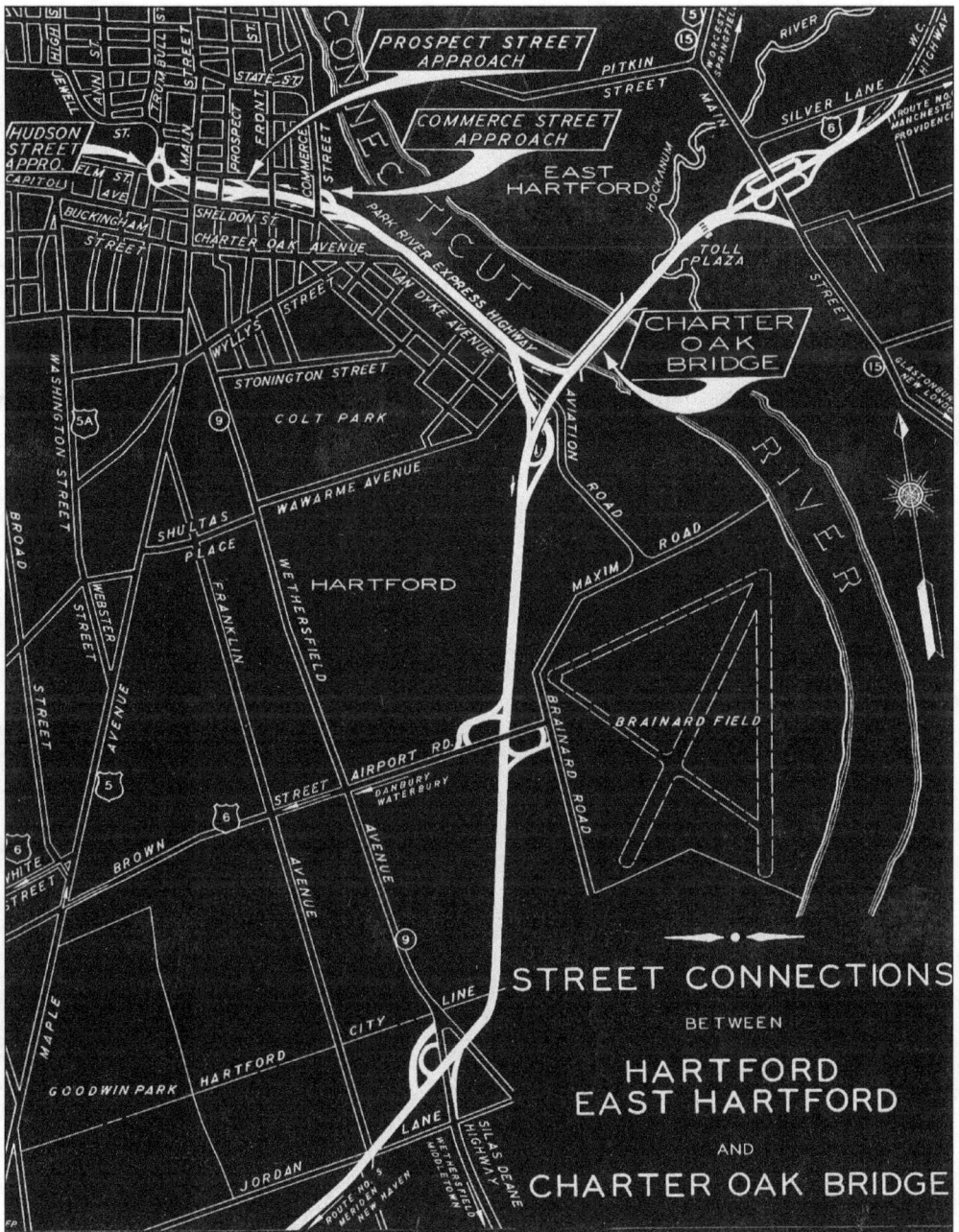

STREET CONNECTIONS. This interesting map showing street connections between Hartford and East Hartford was prepared during 1946 as construction was nearing completion of the Park River Express Highway. The Hartford Bypass is shown leading from below Jordan Lane in Wethersfield to the Charter Oak Bridge. During later years, the bypass became the South Meadows Expressway.

75

A City Landmark. The famous Charter Oak is seen cast into the Charter Oak Bridge railing in this view, which looks east toward East Hartford. On September 16, 1948, the bridge received first prize in the Artistic Bridge Awards competition of the American Institute of Steel Construction. Dr. David B. Steinman of Robinson and Steinman accepted the award on behalf of the consulting firm and the Connecticut State Highway Department. Steinman was retained for the design and contract plans, and he acted as consultant during construction by

the American Bridge Company. Steinman had received previous awards for the Henry Hudson Bridge over Spuyten Duyvil in New York, the Mount Hope Bridge over Narragansett Bay in Rhode Island, the Waldo Bridge over the Penobscot River in Maine, and the Thousand Islands Bridge over the St. Lawrence River. At the time he received the award for the Charter Oak Bridge, he had been retained as a consulting engineer, planning the reconstruction of the Brooklyn Bridge.

THE LEADER OF THE CONNECTICUT HIGHWAY DEPARTMENT. Col. Howard S. Ives is shown being interviewed by a reporter from WTIC radio during 1963. Ives served as the seventh Connecticut State Highway Department commissioner from 1959 to 1969. He spearheaded the effort to ensure completion of the Connecticut sections of the National Defense Highway System. Interstate 91 became a high priority for Ives, as he recognized the need for alleviating traffic congestion along Route 15 from Meriden to Hartford.

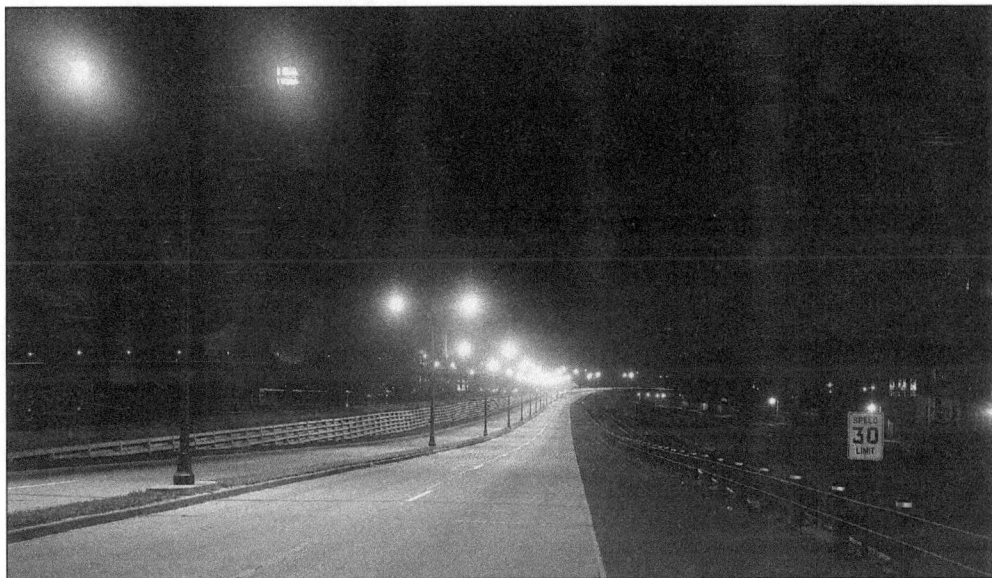

MINIMAL TRAFFIC. Connecticut River Boulevard is seen in this night view taken late in 1947. The Dutch Point Generating Station of the Hartford Electric Light Company is visible in the center. The Connecticut River flows to the left, with lights equally spaced on the Charter Oak Bridge.

NIGHTSCAPE. The Charter Oak Bridge practically glows in the dark from sodium vapor lamps located in the center island. When the Charter Oak Bridge opened during 1942, only low-level temporary lighting was provided. The threat of an attack by air convinced project planners to defer the permanent lighting until the conclusion of hostilities.

RAILING DECORATION. The Charter Oak Bridge, the Hartford Bypass, and the Park River Express Highway were designed as a single highway-improvement project. George Dunkelberger's artistic talents were used for embellishing the bridge railings on the project. He was fond of local history and included this interest in designing four unique railing medallions. The aviation medallion is shown above in the Route 5–Main Street underpass in East Hartford.

THE CHARTER OAK. Medallion number one features a silhouette of the Charter Oak. During 1687, a turbulent period in Connecticut's colonial history, Joseph Wadsworth secreted Connecticut's charter, granted by King Charles II, in the hollow of an oak tree. The oak tree, located on property owned by Samuel Wyllys (Wyllys Street), earned the name Charter Oak and became the namesake of the Charter Oak Bridge.

THE OLD STATEHOUSE.
Medallion number two
silhouettes the old statehouse
in Hartford, a landmark
designed by Charles Bulfinch,
an architect who also designed
the statehouse in Boston. The
old statehouse reflects the
civic architecture of the early
Federal period. Constructed
during 1796, it was the
seat of early Connecticut
government, containing the
secretary of state's office,
legislative chambers, and
the Supreme Court room.

THE FIRST
CONGREGATIONAL
CHURCH. Medallion
number three silhouettes
the First Congregational
Church at Church
Corners in East Hartford.
Constructed during
1836 as East Hartford's
town hall, this imposing
building stands at the
corner of Main Street and
Connecticut Boulevard.

EAST HARTFORD AVIATION. Medallion number four silhouettes the East Hartford aviation industry. When George Dunkelberger created the drawing for this medallion, American Airlines used nearby Rentschler Field on its regular service to Boston and New York. Local aviation industries included Pratt and Whitney Aircraft Works, Chance Voight Corporation, and Hamilton Standard Propeller Company.

THE TOLL PLAZA. The Charter Oak Bridge toll plaza included eight booths and an administration building. When the bridge opened on September 5, 1942, wood booths were used temporarily by toll takers for six months until war-restricted materials became available for constructing permanent booths. The Charter Oak toll station remained in operation for 47 years until 1989, when the bridge became toll-free.

TOLL COLLECTORS. The first female toll collectors in the United States were employed by the Hartford Bridge Authority at the Charter Oak toll station. Shown in September 1942 are, from left to right, Ruth Cashman, Mary Ann Porter, Helen Peter, and Theresa Kenny.

WAITING FOR CUSTOMERS. Mary Ann Porter stands ready to receive a toll during August 1943 at the height of World War II. With gasoline rationing in effect, traffic was practically nonexistent except for those traveling to and from work and commercial trucks carrying materials for the war effort.

Tariff and Traffic Regulations

Charter Oak Bridge
Hartford Bridge Commission
Hartford, Connecticut

Toll Rates

Basic rate	5¢ per axle
Passenger automobiles (2 axle)	10¢
Passenger automobiles with trailer	5¢ per axle
Taxicabs	10¢
Commercial cars and trucks	5¢ per axle
Passenger bus	5¢ per axle
Horse drawn vehicles	10¢
Horse and rider	10¢
Motorcycle	10¢
Bicycle	10¢

Commutation Rates

Commutation rates are available to daily users of the bridge, operating two axle passenger automobiles registered as passenger, combination passenger and commercial, dealer's passenger, repairer's passenger, livery passenger and taxicabs. Sixty (60) trip ticket books costing $3.00 and limited for 30 day use are on sale at the bridge.

Accommodation Ticket Books

Containing coupons good for fifty trips, shall be available for sale to frequent users at regular toll rates on application to the bridge office.

Speed Limits

25 miles per hour on the bridge.

All commercial vehicles must use toll lane posted for passage of commercial traffic.

All vehicles using the bridge must slow down approaching toll station and come to a complete stop in toll lane for the payment of toll.

Weight and Size Limitations

Weight and size of vehicles is limited as provided in the Statutes of the State of Connecticut.

Special permits, issued by the State Highway Commissioner, will be required of all vehicles that exceed the legal requirements of the State of Connecticut.

Parking

No parking will be permitted on the Bridge or its approaches.

HARTFORD BRIDGE COMMISSION.

TOLL RATES. The tariff and traffic regulations written for the Charter Oak Bridge during 1942 included horse-drawn vehicles and horse-and-rider at 10¢. Free passage was limited to bridge employees, members of the bridge commission, police and fire employees, and Connecticut State Highway Department vehicles.

THE ICE PATROL. The Connecticut State Highway Department was responsible for maintaining safe roadways on the Charter Oak Bridge. Nationally recognized for its snow-removal efforts, the department faced the daunting task of winter maintenance on state roads along the shoreline and in the western hills. This view, taken during 1947, shows a sanding truck ready to go as Ice Patrol Unit No 1.

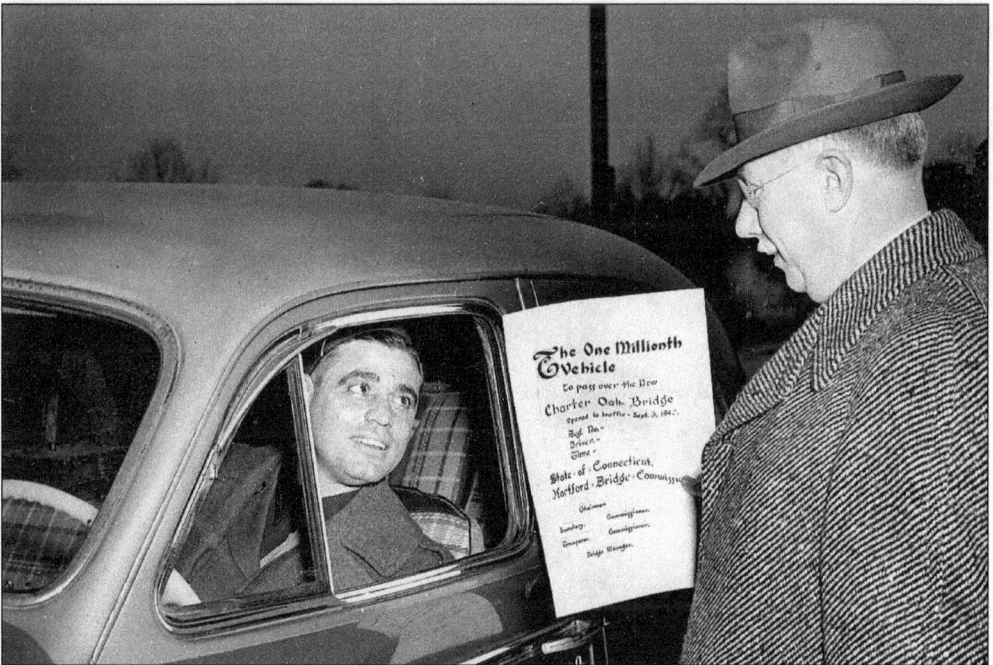

A MILESTONE. William B. Griffin, Charter Oak Bridge manager, is shown on March 20, 1943, presenting Pvt. Frank Anderson of Swampscott, Massachusetts, a certificate honoring his car as the millionth vehicle to cross the bridge.

85

HIGH WATER. The old statehouse is captured in this photograph of a railing medallion on the northwest viaduct of the Charter Oak Bridge. This portion of the bridge was not opened to traffic until late 1946, following the delayed completion of the Park River Express Highway.

SLED TEAM. Cecil "Mush" Moore of Lewiston, Maine, is about to cross the Charter Oak Bridge with his rolling sled and team of nine huskies during 1951. He was heading home to Maine after a 16-month trip to Fairbanks, Alaska. According to Mush, more miles were covered by the sled runners in the snows of the far north than were covered by the wheels in the lower 48 states.

86

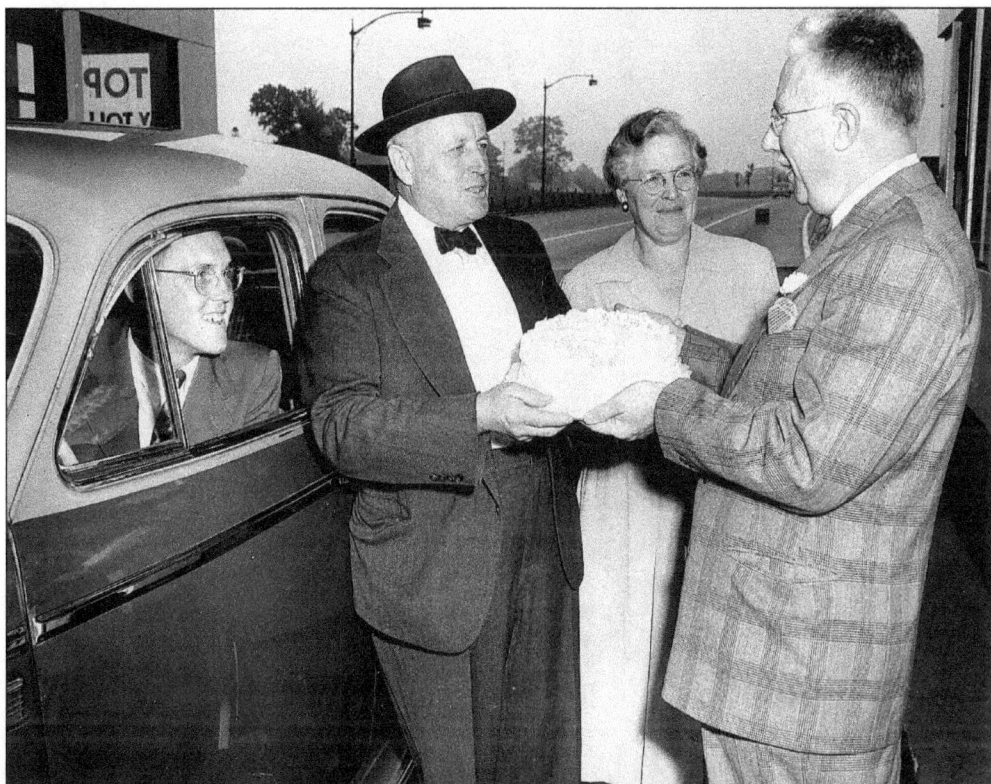

A SECOND MILESTONE. William B. Griffin, Charter Oak Bridge manager, is shown presenting a cake to the Pantaleo family on September 11, 1943. Their car, driven by son Louis Pantaleo, was the two-millionth vehicle to cross the one-year-old Charter Oak Bridge. Toll revenues by this point had exceeded $200,000. The bridge was constructed at a cost of $2 million.

THE ROAD TO HARTFORD. The Hartford Bypass ended at this point with the driver making a decision to either travel over the Charter Oak Bridge or take the ramp to the right that led to Connecticut River Boulevard. At this point of 1947, no route number existed for the road to Hartford. Motorists depended upon place names and road names for guidance from Greenwich to Union.

THREE SISTERS. Three bridges crossing the Connecticut River appear in this 1957 photograph. The Charter Oak Bridge is seen at the top, just below the Dutch Point Generating Station; the Founders Bridge is under construction; and the Bulkeley Bridge is to be widened during 1964 to carry Interstate 84. Most of the buildings seen at center right would become memories with the eventual construction of Constitution Plaza. During 1957, plans were being prepared to construct Interstate 91 along the river. The photograph shows the future ramp connections from the unfinished Founders Bridge to Interstate 91.

Five

THE WILBUR CROSS HIGHWAY

The Wilbur Cross Highway is the only road in Connecticut originally planned as a parkway and finally constructed as an interstate. It was included as a future parkway in Connecticut's comprehensive parkway system during the 1930s. The Wilbur Cross Parkway (Cross Parkway) was planned to span the state from Milford to Union and include tolls at Union. By 1940, a two-lane section of the Cross Parkway had been actually constructed through Willington, Ashford, and part of Union. With the advent of World War II, plans for the Cross Parkway were changed to a full-use limited-access highway that in future years became the footprint for Interstate 86, followed by Interstate 84. After World War II, the 25-mile gap between East Hartford and Tolland Station was constructed as a four-lane divided highway. Two additional lanes were added from Tolland Station to the Massachusetts state line by 1954. At last, a dual-lane route extending 117 miles from Greenwich to Union was completed. However, by 1954, the Commonwealth of Massachusetts was preparing plans for the Massachusetts Turnpike, a toll road with interstate status as the replacement for outdated U.S. Route 20. An exit at Sturbridge connected the Massachusetts Turnpike to the Wilbur Cross Highway. Within 20 years, the Wilbur Cross Highway was obsolete, having been affected by a shift in regional traffic patterns and volumes.

A VIEW TO THE EAST. A 1946 aerial view of the Charter Oak Bridge and toll plaza shows the U.S. Route 5 cloverleaf at the Charter Oak Bridge approach in East Hartford. Also visible are the stubs for connecting the future Wilbur Cross Highway to the northeast. To the right is the sprawling United Aircraft Corporation and Rentschler Field.

APPROACHING THE CHARTER OAK BRIDGE. This view shows traffic approaching the Charter Oak Bridge from the Wilbur Cross Highway during 1950. An East Hartford tobacco shed is visible to the left, a relic from a time when Connecticut Valley shade-grown tobacco was produced where the highway was constructed. Ramps connecting the Wilbur Cross Highway to U.S. Route 5 are shown in the center.

DISTINCTIVE RAILINGS. In this 1948 view looking north, the single-span, rigid-frame bridge carries the Wilbur Cross Highway over Main Street in East Hartford. Each railing panel exhibits George Dunkelberger's artistic talent. The facing-side railing includes the First Congregational Church medallions and the opposite-side railing includes the East Hartford aviation industry medallions.

SPEEDING VIOLATION. A hapless Connecticut motorist in his 1941 Chevrolet receives a speeding citation from a state trooper at the east end of the Charter Oak Bridge during 1952. Speeding on the Charter Oak Bridge and its approaches was closely monitored following a 1951 accident when two Hartford-area women were killed as their car plunged through the bridge railing and fell 50 feet to the ground below.

NEW CONSTRUCTION. This early view of the Wilbur Cross Highway was taken during 1948 before the installation of traffic signs and pavement markings. It shows the Forbes Street interchange, looking north. The area to the right became Veterans Memorial Park in later years.

EASY TRAFFIC A twin-span bridge carries Forbes Street in East Hartford over the Wilbur Cross Highway during 1948. This section of the Wilbur Cross Highway was constructed as a dual-lane highway from East Hartford to Tolland Station. Bridges constructed in Connecticut following World War II lacked the imaginative designs of their prewar counterparts. A greater emphasis was placed on utility of purpose following the guidelines of federal aid participation.

A REAL GEM. A 1946 Chevrolet passes through the Buckland Street overpass during 1952. Faced with random ashlar stone, this bridge, with curved wing walls, was unusual for the Wilbur Cross Highway. It was demolished when Interstate 84 replaced Route 15 from East Hartford to Union. Stone-faced bridges were a rarity on the Route 15 corridor from Greenwich to Union.

AROUND THE ROTARY. The busy intersection of Main Street and East Center Street in Manchester included this rotary during 1946. A 1939 Pontiac and a 1940 Ford panel truck navigate the rotary in front of the Manchester Post Office. To the right is a 1937 Chevrolet coupe. Main Street to the north was a major connector to the Wilbur Cross Highway.

SERVICE AHEAD. An advance information shingle-edged sign located near Vernon provides assurance that Flying A service is just ahead. Shingle-edged signing was a standard for the Route 15 corridor. First used on the Merritt Parkway, the signs were unique and projected a rustic appearance. In 1941, Montclair, New Jersey, and Hagerstown, Maryland, were granted permission by the Connecticut State Highway Department to use the same design.

GASSING UP. A 1949 DeSoto is being serviced at the southbound Wilbur Cross Highway gasoline station in Vernon during the summer of 1956. The period pump globes advertise Cities Service gasoline, and the white window shutters exhibit silhouetted pine trees. To the right, a panel truck waits to assist a stranded driver along Route 15.

A HIGHWAY CREW. Connecticut state highways were considered among the nation's best during the 1940s and 1950s highway era. Shown above is a Wilbur Cross Highway maintenance crew who plowed snow in the winter and mowed grass in the summer. The crew was led by Rudolph Supina, shown standing at left, during 1948. He at one time was the executive head of Highway Maintenance for Connecticut's state highway system.

HEADING FOR MASSACHUSETTS. The northern end of Route 15 is shown extending from Wallingford, Connecticut, to Sturbridge, Massachusetts. At this point, Route 15 joined U.S. Route 20, stretching from Boston to Newport, Oregon. The Wilbur Cross Highway in northern Connecticut was originally constructed only two lanes wide. Later, as traffic demands increased, the road was widened to four lanes with a divider strip. The eastern 15 miles of Route 15 required constant monitoring for winter snow and icing conditions. It passed through a near wilderness of undeveloped countryside. The ribbon of road from Greenwich to Union, stretching 117 miles, fulfilled the best intentions of James H. MacDonald, pioneer of highways.

www.ingramcontent.com/pod-product-compliance
Lightning Source LLC
Chambersburg PA
CBHW050614110426
42813CB00008B/2556